YOUR PERSONALITY REVEALED:

SELF-ANALYSIS THROUGH HANDWRITING

GLORIA HARGREAVES

YOUR PERSONALITY REVEALED:

SELF-ANALYSIS THROUGH HANDWRITING

PETER OWEN • LONDON & CHESTER SPRINGS

For Peggy, whose help is
invaluable; Janet, Anne,
Gillian, Pamela, Jenny and
Marabelle, who have assisted
me on my lecture tours
around the world

PETER OWEN PUBLISHERS
73 Kenway Road London SW5 ORE

Peter Owen books are distributed in the USA by
Dufour Editions Inc. Chester Springs PA
19425-0007

This edition first published in Great Britain 1996
© Gloria Hargreaves 1996

A catalogue record for this book is available
from the British Library

ISBN 0-7206-0997-6

Printed in Great Britain by
Biddles of Guildford and King's Lynn

CONTENTS

INTRODUCTION

How do you function in your chosen career? Are you a good decision maker? Do you have leadership qualities? What is your attention to detail like? In personal relationships, do you consider your partner's feelings? Perhaps you are the happy-go-lucky type, but does this pay the bills? Do you consider your children a joy and pleasure, or are they getting in the way of your doing just what you want to do? Are you creative, do you enjoy sport, or are you the greatest of lovers?

Have you been making accurate assessments of yourself and others? You may have been amazed when others have let you down when you have always considered yourself such a good judge of character. Perhaps, at times, your own actions or reactions amaze you.

It is time to rediscover who you really are and what motivates you. The human personality is extremely complex and one of the greatest aids to understanding oneself and others is handwriting analysis. Now you can analyse your own handwriting.

Graphology, or handwriting analysis, is the study of handwriting movements for the purpose of determining the personality of the writer. No two people write exactly the same – even twins write differently.

Handwriting is actually brainwriting; we merely use our hands as a tool to produce our particular script. There has been for many years now an established body of knowledge on which handwriting analysis is based and the same rules are applied worldwide.

Age cannot be determined with total accuracy. A person's actual age is often at variance with his mental age – you meet mature 14-year-olds and immature 50-year-olds! The sex of a person is another difficult area to determine, as we all have masculine as well as feminine traits in our makeup.

Left-handedness makes little difference, since as many lefthanders as righthanders produce a right slanting script. Perhaps you have noticed how they adjust the paper, or their position, in order to do this. People who have lost the use of one hand and are forced to use the other generally develop a writing style that closely resembles their earlier one, unless of course their personality has changed. Graphology is not predictive but it can clearly show your potential.

Fast handwriting suggests a greater degree of naturalness, genuineness and spontaneity; while slow writing, in an adult, reveals a more self-conscious, calculating personality.

This book is divided into two sections. Section I sets out the interpretations of the dominant movements. These are the movements that immediately strike you as you look at a sample. Section II gives interpretations of the secondary, or lesser movements. These will be evident on closer inspection of the writing. A movement that appears occasionally shows a tendency; if it appears often it shows a habit. And, if it appears constantly, it is an integral part of the personality. The human personality is full of contradictions and you may find that some of the interpretations are too. But this is simply an indication that no one is totally extrovert or totally introvert; completely selfish or unselfish, but that we are all made up of a mixture of positive and negative traits. As a result, no one should ever be afraid of having their handwriting analysed – we are each as good as the next person, just different.

All you need to do to get the maximum benefit from this book is to:

1) produce a sample of handwriting on unlined paper (approximately 50 words is ideal);
2) choose the dominant movements from Section I that immediately strike you on looking at the sample;
3) choose the secondary movements from Section II

8

that you find on closer inspection;
4) combine the two for the analysis that is
uniquely yours.

It is preferable to use a sample not specifically written for this exercise and produced with the pen the writer is most comfortable with.

THE FOLLOWING ARE EXAMPLES OF SCRIPTS
WITH THEIR DOMINANT AND SECONDARY
MOVEMENTS INDICATED.

Curiosity causes me to write this note for your handwriting expert.

1. **Large size.** *Dominant lower zone. Right slant. Triangular g and y. Long t crosses.*

is extraordinarily good when not

2. **Totally disconnected.** *Pasty pressure. Accurate i dots. o's open to right.*

I enclose a sample of my handwriting which I'd like you to analyse, and, I enclose a

3. **Angular letter shapes.** *Connected. Single stroke personal pronoun 'I'. Accurate i dots.*

9

all quite silly but I
splitting to have to do
with the way I read

4. **Varying sized letters.** *Uneven baseline. Very small personal pronoun 'I'. Loops on t's.*

To tell you a little
my own personality -
am an introvent or a

5. **Arcade letter shapes.** *Dominant middle zone. Words too close together. i dots to right.*

The quick brown fox
jumped over the lazy
dog.

6. **Balanced zones.** Garland letter shapes. Simplified writing style. Good word and line spacing.

SECTION I

Dominant Movements

1

Size

Size	3 mm
	3 mm
	3 mm
large	9½ mm plus
medium	9 mm
small	8½ mm or less
Varying size	

I am having a drink
bar; now I have th

If you have large handwriting, you are extroverted, extravagant and must excel in whatever you do. The intensity of your drive is greater the larger your script. You have strong feelings of self-importance and are prone to bouts of exhibitionism. You are very imaginative, need variety and plenty of activity. You also have a yearning for power and the desire to dominate others. Your leadership qualities are considerable and material possessions mean a great deal to you. On the negative side, you can be too bossy, inattentive to detail, and absent-minded. Your extravagance can get you into financial difficulty and your constant need for a new challenge makes you restless, careless and often tactless.

In business   You are only comfortable in the boss's seat, have fine leadership qualities and are never short of new ideas. You will command respect and can be intolerant of others who do not match up to the standards you set for them.

As a lover   You are great: imaginative, and fond of variety. You do everything on a grand scale and are likely to whisk a lover off to Paris or Rome for a quick lunch! You love buying expensive gifts, and you expect the same in return. When life becomes dull or boring with a particular partner who is not adventurous, you do have the tendency to move on!

As a parent   You want the very best for your children and will encourage and praise them when they do well. Money will always be made available for extra activities, such as horse riding, skiing, school outings and dance classes. It is always a two-way deal with you: you do your best; we'll give you the means to do it!

MEDIUM

What a lovely party!
did so enjoy it all.
you must have worked

If you have a medium-sized script, you tend to be conventional and fit in with prevailing circumstances. You

13

neither over- nor underestimate your own abilities. Too much responsibility is unwelcome and you are most comfortable in a position as second-in-command, or as an assistant. You find a certain amount of routine appealing and your mind is rarely divorced from reality. You are usually practical and realistic, with your feet firmly on the ground, but sometimes you limit yourself and could explore life more fully.

In business A doer rather than a thinker, you would make an excellent personal assistant – no one need worry that you are after their job! You are frequently delightful and pleasant to all around you, unless pushed to do what you consider is beyond your capabilities or sphere of responsibility. You need a degree of comfort and steadiness in everything you do.

As a lover Security comes high on your list of priorities. You like the 'tried and trusted' and tend to stay with one partner as long as life is reasonably comfortable. Friday-night sex after the pub on a weekly basis could well be acceptable to you. You are not necessarily boring but like planning and organization in your life. Extravagant gestures have little appeal but genuine acts of kindness are greatly appreciated. You show great respect to a good provider.

As a parent On the whole, you are a good parent, since your kind disposition makes you conscious of your children's needs. You encourage a child to do his/her best and set no hard or fast rules. You will show extreme pride if one of your offspring does particularly well in anything. On the whole, yours is a comfortable family situation.

Mary had a little lamb
Its fleece was white as snow
And everywhere that Mary went
The lamb was sure to go

Small writing is that of shy and modest people who rarely seek the limelight and can be somewhat introverted. Very realistic, and with great powers of concentration, you relate best to those well known to you but are cautious with strangers. Your emotions are controlled and self-discipline is strongly in evidence. You are contemplative and reflective. You approach life intellectually, and with great attention to detail. You may show considerable executive ability but often need the leadership qualities shown by the large handwriter to put your ideas to maximum effect. You can be quite independent of what others think.

In business Your capacity for accuracy and aptitude, for detailed, scientific work makes you invaluable, as does your ability to work alone for long periods of time on a project. You also work extremely well in areas where confidentiality and loyalty are important. You will always exhibit a very well-developed sense of economy.

As a lover Not overly imaginative but tender and thoughtful, you have a strong tendency to discipline impulses and emotions, so a sensual and loving partner can be of immense help to your controlled personality. Loyalty rates highly, so you rarely run off with the lover of your best friend! As a small writer, you loathe your partner giving away intimate details of your personal relationship, so your partner will have to learn not to discuss you with others. You also frown on public displays of affection. Small, well-chosen gifts are the order of the day for you.

As a parent Praising your offspring does not come naturally to you, since you can often feel overrated yourself when given genuine praise and believe the same applies to your children. You do not like parting with your money, so you won't necessarily provide designer jeans or trainers, unless of course they will last for many years. However, you will invariably provide money for whatever you consider wise and of long-term benefit to your offspring, such as exchange visits with other students. You encourage academic pursuits and exude a quiet air of approval – sometimes!

VARYING

I am not in a good mood
But I might be better later
Hope So

You can be very charming but also very erratic – one day full of ideas, the next day unimaginative, dull and boring. Frequently you exhibit childish behaviour and may often feel off-balance, both personally and professionally. You long for success one moment and welcome the mundane the next. You can be very talkative one moment and silent the next. Your dominant traits will be self-centredness and moodiness.

In business There is a strong tendency to drive those around you to distraction. You will praise their ideas one moment and deny they even made a suggestion the next; worse still, you may even claim someone else's brilliant idea as your own. Very difficult to pin down to a particular course of action, you are likely to change arrangements at the last moment. Your intermittent charm and great sense of humour rarely compensate for your mood swings and inconsistency.

As a lover Your lover may swing from the chandelier tonight and go unnoticed tomorrow: 'I will always love you' and 'What are you hanging around for?' are alternate responses you are likely to offer them. You will provide excitement, you will cause tears and above all, you will offer uncertainty: giving your lover a diamond ring today and forgetting that all-important anniversary tomorrow. Your lover will need a lot of patience to deal with you!

As a parent Bouts of absolute adoration and praise for your children are followed by frustration: 'The children are getting under my feet, can't you control them?' You need a very stable partner, one who will make up for the times that you fail to meet promises or obligations. At times, you will ply your children with wonderful, expensive gifts, but these can be inappropriate and to your liking rather than your children's. Although undisciplined, you are also very entertaining and amusing, younger children tend to adore you and see only what is good. As they mature, they may well wonder whether you were always so unreliable.

2

Zone Sizes

balanced zones

dominant upper ←

dominant middle ←

dominant lower zone ←

BALANCED

act of writing — 1.
Thought I would to
chose, but trying s
I fuss about havi

If you stick to the copybook proportions, you have a balanced outlook, with an equal focus on the three dominant areas: intellectual, social and instinctual. You are a happy person with inner harmony. There is no exaggerated trait, and you generally progress through life with a contented attitude and wholesome self-confidence.

In business   As you rarely over- or underestimate your own abilities, you tend to find employment that will neither push you beyond your abilities nor hold you back. You believe in fair pay for a good day's work and will resist anyone taking advantage of you. Fairness, loyalty and reliability are all characteristic of you as a worker. You may not set the world alight, but you won't be lost in the crowd. You will fight for the rights of your fellow-workers and would make a good union leader or supervisor. Your energy level is good and you pace yourself very well indeed.

As a lover   Your partner and family mean a great deal to you, and you give the same attention to your family responsibilities that you do to your business commitments. You like a well-kept home and are quite happy to help with the household tasks. Fairness rates very highly with you and you are more than happy to 'pull your weight'. You are a good provider and are very loyal to your partner. A good standard of living is important to you, and you enjoy luxuries but do not need them. Sexually, you are considerate and active.

As a parent   You are the nice, solid type who enjoys family life. You praise and encourage your children when appropriate but also insist that they make their contribution, whether it be helping with the housework, doing their share of the cooking or eventually contributing to the expenses. You encourage your children to grow, develop and become responsible adults, and you promote a healthy environment.

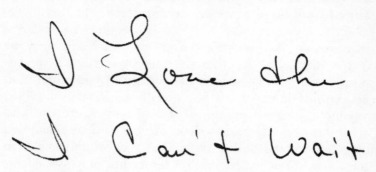

Basically, your interests are of an intellectual and possibly spiritual nature. You are a person with high ideals and aspirations but little interest in everyday commitments. There are no solid foundations to your personality and your endeavours may not be rooted in reality. Your active imagination is allied to idealism and the tendency to daydream. Often very well-read, with an interest in all the arts, you can be insufficiently down-to-earth to know what you really want from life.

In business A 'good-ideas' person, you need the help of colleagues for your ideas to reach fruition. You show a lot of ambition, but become very disillusioned when others do not reach the high standards you consider acceptable. You are very proud and take offence quite easily. You can be very critical of yourself and others and are not the most cheerful person to work with. Under pressure you tend to flee to your active dream life.

As a lover You will take your lover to concerts, the theatre and movies but will be very critical of what you see. As your feet are not firmly on the ground, you can mislead your partner as to your earning capacity, status in society, and so on, so don't be surprised if others don't believe everything they are told! With your uncompromising ideas of what is right and what is wrong, you are easily upset, so others must be on their best behaviour at all times. You are not very cheerful and things must be just right to put you in a sexual frame of mind. Although you have a good imagination, you are always frightened of doing the 'wrong' thing sexually.

As a parent   Strict and uncompromising, you expect your children to do their very best at all times, and you will be very disappointed if they do not attain top grades in all their subjects. You are not tactile, so children can feel unloved unless their other parent is warm and affectionate. You show little interest in the children's social life and will discourage much interaction with friends and neighbours. You lack a sense of humour.

DOMINANT MIDDLE ZONE

*for your helpful
I'm looking forward
handwriting samples!*

You live for today – what is happening now is what is important – and you are very self-involved. Teenagers, who think of nothing more than their own daily activities, commonly exhibit this writing style. Often strong-willed and self-reliant, with a big ego, you want excitement on a daily basis and have difficulty in delaying pleasure. You can be most inconsiderate of the needs of others but seem completely unaware of it. Your conceit can be great and you can make a big deal of trivia.

In business   You frequently want to be the leader and you do have some leadership qualities, but you tell others what to do rather than ask, and want things done your way. Your presumptuousness is very difficult to handle and you tend to antagonize those who work with you. At times you are lazy and can indulge yourself in taking time off for minor reasons.

As a lover A lover may arrive on your doorstep and literally be dragged to the bedroom, since you have difficulty delaying pleasure. You can be hard to satisfy, and repeat performances may be the order of the day. You can also be quite generous, but the whole world will know about it. You welcome and encourage your partners to spend money on you. You can overindulge in eating, drinking and clothes-buying.

As a parent As you are very wrapped up in your own needs you can find great difficulty in handling the needs of a child. However, you will, when it suits you, overindulge them too. You will line up a good array of baby-sitters, friends and relations to help with your children when your own needs take priority. Invariably, you love your kids and will buy them the best and send them to expensive schools, but you are sometimes emotionally unavailable to them.

DOMINANT LOWER ZONE

a little gmb round my tummy a honey pot

Sex, money and sporting interests are what matter to you. You have tremendous physical energy but find it difficult to channel it into productive outlets. At times you will be totally driven by ideas for making money (often quick ways) while at other times you will leave the office at lunch-time to play a round of golf. You may need more than one outlet for your sexual energy or, at best, wear out your partner with your sexual demands. Frequently, your type has many creative ideas but often needs help in carrying them out. Sometimes you are over-emotional.

In business   You are an exciting, exuberant go-getter, but so variable! You may run your own business (hopefully with a small handwriter!) where you do not have to answer to others for your erratic behaviour. When you do push to close a deal, no one will show more energy and drive, particularly when the rewards are very high. But on a day when you do not feel like being in the office, you might as well forget it. You are whimsical, may lack maturity, but you are also charming, and can reach great heights of success, even if you fall flat on your face a number of times *en route*! You are a bad timekeeper and one of your favourite sayings is 'the cheque is in the post'.

As a lover   Above all, you are demanding and like variety. You want all the good things in life: expensive restaurants, being seen in the best holiday spots with a sexy, very attractive partner in tow, fast cars, designer labels, a detached home (preferably with a swimming pool and space for four cars). You often live above your means but do not feel too much guilt about this. Life for your lover will never be boring, but it can be worrying. You just might abandon your partner for one of their beautiful friends!

As a parent   You may be quite doting, but you won't always keep your promises. In due time your children will get what they want, but as and when it is convenient for you. You love showing off your children and will ensure that they always look wonderful. The children will also flaunt designer labels and the latest toys; what they often miss out on is time and attention, which can come at a premium with you and compete with your other activities.

3

Slant

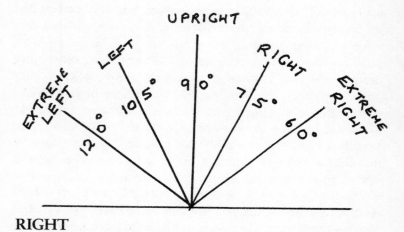

UPRIGHT

LEFT

RIGHT

EXTREME LEFT

EXTREME RIGHT

120°

105°

90°

75°

60°

RIGHT

*Such a beautiful cruise.
Such a pretty lady!
Tomorrow Gibralter!!*

You have a friendly, affectionate nature, capable of communicating feelings and ideas to others. You are emotionally responsive and demonstrative, and look to the future with positive ideas. You respond to others in a sympathetic manner and experience no difficulty in getting along with them. You have a genuine social quality, enjoy entertaining others and being entertained by them. You tend to hold on to friends for many years and are at your best

24

when surrounded by other people. You are a very progressive thinker. You dislike long periods of time alone.

In business   The ability to communicate easily and well tends to draw your type towards sales and marketing positions, or any position where direct contact is a strong requirement. You love forward planning in everything and can become restless if you have nothing new and demanding to look forward to. You work hard and enthusiastically.

As a lover   You are delightful, charming, romantic, caring and easy to get along with. Your affectionate personality enables you to attract others easily. A good and active social life is necessary, both in and outside the home. You are capable of warmth and variety in your sex life, and you readily give unexpected gifts and perform acts of kindness.

As a parent   Again, you are caring, demonstrative and communicative, always ready with a listening ear and prepared to encourage and praise your offspring. You look on life as one big adventure and encourage your children to do likewise. Enquiring, enterprising and enthusiastic, you consider anything and everything worth sharing; for you it is paramount that the family enjoy things together in a good family environment.

EXTREME RIGHT

I have pleasure in enclosing a cheque of premium paid in respect of the

Over the top! You are constantly crying or laughing, very impulsive and in need of constant change and variety. You are terribly enthusiastic about new ideas and always dashing from one to the other, without understanding why others are more controlled. You can miss out on the good things of today for the dreams of tomorrow. You do communicate but your listener must have a lot of time to spare as you do not know when to stop your 'ear-bashing'. You can become hysterical under pressure and may wear yourself out at an early age.

In business Too rash by far, you need a really tight rein to keep you steady. You tend to move on to new ideas before getting the maximum out of existing ones. Impatient with colleagues and customers, you will exaggerate stories beyond all recognition. Yours is a theatrical personality and you join causes on impulse. You can make an extremely successful salesperson, but others won't be able to believe all you tell them!

As a lover You are the 'head over heels at first sight' type, and you require undivided attention at all times. You are very demonstrative anywhere, but you also tend to be extremely jealous and possessive. You must be fed on large doses of charm, flattery and sex. You hate being left alone even for reasonably short periods of time, for you consider this neglect, and can behave in a quite resentful fashion. Your romantic impulses are ardent, demanding and overpowering; this can be flattering initially, but difficult to cope with over the long run.

As a parent 'My child is the best', 'My child does not tell lies' – sound familiar? Everything about your children is beyond criticism in public and it is very difficult for children in this situation to get a balanced view of what is good or bad, right or wrong. At other times you go to the other extreme and punish the child excessively for actual or imagined misdemeanours within the home. It is important to you to project an image of the 'perfect' family, and you display group family photos around your home. You are too extreme to come anywhere close to a model parent.

Now is the time
to the aid of th
The quick brow
jumped over the t

This example shows a balance between the mind and the emotions. Your character is generally reserved, with a dry sense of humour. Your responses are cautious, considered and to-the-point. You have the ability to accept the responsibilities of life and regard them with a dedicated calmness. You have a very independent personality and would make a good planner or organizer. At times you may appear cold, calculating and sceptical. You are loyal, honest, self-controlled and live in the present moment.

In business   Your loyalty and self-reliance are without question the most entrenched of all the personality-types. Likewise, your impartial attitudes and independent thinking can be invaluable. You can make an excellent leader or equally contented loner, and your ability to remain calm when everything is falling down around you is unequalled. However, you loathe criticism and will give up on a task if anyone suggests that you are unable to carry it out properly.

As a lover   You show your loyalty with everyday acts of kindness and consideration. Your emotions are kept in check and you take a long time to give your total commitment. But once committed, you hang on to what is dear to you for life. Fickleness is not a feature of your personality type and you welcome the responsibility of home life. In arguing a point, you will appeal to logic rather than emotion. You are a good, solid, steadfast lover – perhaps not the most romantic but the most sustaining. You always remember birthdays and anniversaries, and tend to give practical gifts.

As a parent You enjoy the responsibilities and joys of family life, so take to it easily. You give praise where praise is due and encourage, or even criticize where necessary. You can be a very caring parent who will take the time and trouble to explain things to your offspring. You are likely to make outings to museums and art galleries, and will not spoil or overinduldge. You encourage your children to think for themselves and make decisions independently. Kisses and affection are not abundant but are given spontaneously when required.

LEFT

relevant off-the-job train
It is important that each
co-ordinated and it is su
Agent' he is responsible
Financial support to emplo.

Your two most dominant traits are caution and sensitivity. You can be quite passive and may even display defensive and negative attitudes, but once you overcome your initial caution, you move forward with much determination. Sensitivity does play a big part in how much risk-taking you will consider. You fear ridicule and tend to hide your emotions, possibly displaying a well-constructed front to cover up and compensate for inner feelings of withdrawal. You often repress feelings and can become very anxious and fearful in new situations. As a left-slanter you tend to resist change or progress and will stay in the same job for many years rather than risk the challenge of a new environment. (In many cases of left-slanting handwriting, the mother has played a dominant role and the positive male identification is jeopardized.) However, there are many highly successful left-slanters who learn eventually to cut from their past and, although they will never be as relaxed as right-slanters, they do adapt.

In business You would make a very good historian, or excel in a job that involves research or anything relating to the past, such as antique-collecting or dealing. You can be very self-centred and selfish, and thus experience some difficulty in getting along with others. You may seek a position of a solitary nature and can work very well when on your own.

As a lover Slow and cautious, you may be the sort to marry late in life, but if you do give your affections to another you are theirs for life. You need constant reassurance that you are the one and only and can be very selfish in your demands for affection. However, you seldom return these displays of affection and can leave a partner feeling frustrated and angry. You may have had a very close relationship with your mother (or mother-figure), and may well take her on holiday or on shopping expeditions; you need a tolerant partner. You generally don't mix well and prefer the company of those close to you or a small circle of friends.

As a parent Your caution rises strongly to the surface, and you want your children to do *safe* things – take safe jobs and stay close to home. Praise doesn't come easy but criticism does. You will always say 'it is for your own good', but this can be extremely difficult to take and lead to shy, secretive and retiring offspring. You also worry unnecessarily about the health of your children, taking preventative measures which may be unwarranted.

EXTREME LEFT

extreme Left is rarely found and suggests extreme caution in everything one does.

This slant appears very rarely, and the traits described above will apply but heightened to the extreme.

MIXED (right, left and upright)

During my training I became a hairdresser. Finally I gave up.

This is a fascinating script, and surprisingly common. You are subject to swinging moods: happy one minute, dejected and lonely the next. Everything about you is inconsistent and unsettled; your intellect and emotions are in constant conflict – the mind wants to do one thing, the heart another. Common sense and good judgement are lacking and you can become very excitable over trivia. On the positive side, you are always interesting and provocative, and seem to have an inborn ability to relate to many types of personalities.

In business The inconsistency can cause problems and

certainly you experience difficulty in dealing with superiors. You become very nervous and anxious when dealing with people you consider more intelligent than yourself, but in dealing with others who have problems, you come into your own and can be extremely helpful. You can feel socially inferior and off-centre, and often long for a position of responsibility where you will do your utmost to control your capricious nature. My experience has shown that this type often work brilliantly as prison wardens, probation officers and traffic wardens.

As a lover You can be difficult: warm and ardent one moment, cold the next, constantly in need of reassurance, yet doubting that you are worthy of such love. Your emotional nature is so erratic that others never know how you will react to them. You are probably the most difficult partner of all – highly sexed one moment, and completely disinterested at other times. You might walk out at any time and leave your lover for another, but then be surprised if you are not welcomed back with open arms!

As a parent You are not sufficiently consistent in your expressions of love and affection. Children will tend to feel insecure in this environment and wonder if they are to blame for the frequent mood changes; sensitive children may feel inferior and lack confidence. This is a clear case for seeking aid with parenting skills. You are not guilty of unkindness, just inadequate in maintaining the consistency from which most children benefit.

4

Baseline

STRAIGHT

RIGID

VERY UNEVEN

RISING

FALLING

STRAIGHT

A very Happy Christmas + a happy New Year.

Your script indicates stability; you are not easily upset. Your mind disciplines your emotions and you are not easily swayed by every little event or the expressed thoughts of others. You demonstrate orderliness and dependability.

In business You get your priorities right and are not distracted by events going on around you. You organize yourself well and adhere to all promises, deadlines and commitments. You behave in a very stable manner and are happy to assist others who may ask for your help, or time. You demonstrate emotional stability at all levels.

As a lover You always follow through with any plans made, and you feel extremely uncomfortable if you have to let anyone down, even for a very justifiable reason. If someone has a problem, you are an excellent listener and frequently come up with sound, sensible advice. You are a very caring lover, with as much desire to please as to be pleased.

As a parent You are utterly reliable and will stick to any promise made to your offspring. You need an orderly environment and will not tolerate untidiness or slovenly ways so your children will be expected to do their homework at the right time and keep their areas clean and tidy. You will, however, always be there for them to assist in whatever ways are necessary, and you are flexible in your approach to each of your children.

EXCESSIVELY RIGID

become a hairdresser. Dunr training I have been undecic wether that it was the right career for me. Finally in n third year I have decided this

Your writing shows a desire for control; you may lose your spontaneity and behave in an inhibited manner. You drain your energy through the fear of ever letting others know what you are really like. You may have had a parent who expected you to be 'seen but not heard'. When you do lose your cool, all hell breaks loose, but these times are few and far between.

In business You tend to choose your jobs very carefully and avoid situations where you are greatly exposed to others, or expected to work in a team situation. Always at the back of your mind is the thought: 'They will find out I am not as clever as I claim to be', or 'They just won't like me.' You also greatly fear emotional outbursts, both from yourself and from others.

As a lover You are too inhibited and self-conscious to relax and enjoy the great pleasures that a satisfactory, close sexual relationship can bring. You worry about how you look without your clothes. 'Are my breasts too small/large?' 'Is my penis too small? Will I get an erection?' Very occasionally you say 'sod-it' and have a ball! Once every five years, maybe!

As a parent You restrict your offspring greatly and are frightened of every fresh move they make. They are rarely allowed to travel far from home or spend the night with their school friends. You will teach them to save their pocket-money for a rainy day and behave cautiously in everything they do. You are a kindly parent but very restrictive.

VERY UNEVEN

I feel that my bones are beginning to ache and all the psychopathical treatment has been no good.

You are basically unreliable and lacking in will-power. You make all sorts of promises that you know you cannot keep. Clever and capable, you may nevertheless fail at a job for which you are highly suited. Others will wonder why, but it is because of your inability to apply yourself and your difficulty in sticking to a routine. This applies equally to your hobbies and interests. You can be extremely emotional and, at times, confused.

In business Your lack of reliability often leads to frequent job changes and discontent. You are an erratic time-keeper and an inconsistent problem-solver. You are a victim of your own wavering moods, and although you can be very cheerful and friendly, others do tire of your unpredictability and mood swings.

As a lover Sometimes you are attentive and demonstrative; at other times you show disinterest in everything about you. Sex can be a joy or a disaster. You may shower a lover with gifts one day and borrow money from them the next. You may love and loathe them all at the same time. Even friendships that are soundly based on common interests can become strained because of your fluctuating moods.

As a parent You are just as variable towards your children as you are towards your lover. One day you will play with them and take an interest in them; at other times you may ignore them and insist they stay out of your way. You will overspend on them sometimes and fail to provide them with necessary money at other times. You will make them promises that you have no hope of fulfilling. It is vital to have one reliable partner in this situation.

RISING

Please be kind to me had a very trying day

Your script is a very positive one, which shows that you are optimistic and not easily discouraged. You maintain a hopeful attitude and are genuinely happy in whatever you are doing. You make a very cheery companion and are usually willing to lend a helping hand. You express positive attitudes as well as the desire to succeed. You can, however, be restless and over-excitable at times. You don't enjoy too much routine, but should someone suggest something new and interesting to you, you will quickly stir to action. If the rise is exaggerated, it indicates that too much energy is being expended too widely.

In business You are a go-getter who faces problems head on, a pleasant person who sees life as a challenge. You show cheerfulness in the face of adversity and are invariably positive in everything you undertake. Ambitious, you do not expect everything to be given to you on a plate, and you strive with enthusiasm and a buoyant spirit. On the negative side, your organizational ability can be impaired due to your impatience. Good advice might be to slow down and keep your feet more firmly on the ground.

As a lover You would make a charming companion or lover. More often than not, you are in a good mood or, at least, looking on the bright side. You experience no difficulty in adapting yourself socially and will show consideration, generosity, and pride in your partner. Sexually you are inventive and always a lot of fun. You love treating your partner as special and will choose very thoughtful gifts not just for birthdays or special occasions but at any time.

As a parent Happy, cheerful, bright and encouraging, you will get involved with school committees, sports-day organization, etc. You feel pride and joy in your offspring and are capable of making a very happy home life, where children prosper and produce their best efforts. You will encourage your children to try and try again and any lack of success will not be frowned upon. They will be encouraged to try new and different things until they find something they are good at.

FALLING

career -prosperu. i t -
worry that I would regret
in a way a dead end job
6 months I would tire

This script reveals a pessimistic attitude. You do not become enthusiastic about new ideas and are likely to be sceptical of others who do. You lack drive, initiative and the desire to get pleasure from life, preferring to complain and always adopting negative attitudes. You seem to thrive on disparaging remarks, such as, 'The hot weather kills me' or 'Won't be long till winter's here and we'll all freeze to death!' There is no pleasing you.

In business You may well be very good in your chosen profession, but your type are rarely popular. You nit-pick and tend to blame others if things go wrong, imagining slights and rejection and frequently putting off till tomorrow what could easily be done today. Even when you are praised you feel unworthy, and often cover this up under an arrogant exterior. You may give in before you even try a particular task.

As a lover 'I'm not in the mood tonight, perhaps I shall feel more like it tomorrow' or 'I think I have a headache coming on' – these responses are typical of you. You can easily dampen a lover's ardour and enthusiasm by discussing all your problems, real or imagined, at the wrong moment, leaving them feeling tired and depressed. When others buy you gifts, you immediately suspect that they will be unsuitable, inappropriate or just the wrong colour.

As a parent Your negative attitudes tend to hold your children back in many areas. You may discourage their participation in sports-day events or advise them before a competition that they 'haven't a chance of winning'. Invariably you consider their teachers too modern or too old-fashioned; too strict or too lenient – never just right. One of the commonest remarks in your household could be 'In my day, we didn't ask for money, we went out and earned it'. You are prone to expect too much from your children and to give too little. There is much too much criticism in your household and not enough encouragement.

5

Connectedness/
Disconnectedness

Connected The majority of the letters are joined. Allowance can be made for breaks after capitals and other very occasional breaks.

Connected

Disconnected This writing shows only four letters in a word, or less, written with one continuous stroke.

Disconnected

TOTALLY DISCONNECTED

WORDS SOMETIMES Connected

CONNECTED

simultaneously with the building and including into a revised total ?

You know from the beginning of any project just what you are going to do from start to finish. Your thinking is

39

systematic and logical, and you are normally practical and realistic. You don't trust intuition, and analyse everything. You become very restless if your mind is not constantly stimulated, and you often feel more relaxed doing a cross-word, or any puzzle, rather than doing nothing. Personal problems are difficult for you as you are much better at solving abstract ones. You can be very tactless. There are times when you are so busy thinking about what happened yesterday, or what will happen tomorrow, that you miss the pleasures today has to offer.

In business You have a great capacity for getting things done – but woe betide anyone who interrupts you *en route*: you will cooperate when you have reached a proper stopping point, but only then. You are a good organizer and plan ahead well. You rarely jump to conclusions without first stopping to reason things out, but you can sometimes get bogged down by detail, be pedantic, nit-picking and too self-involved.

As a lover On the whole, you are very sentimental but can lack empathy, unless it is with an ailment you have experienced, e.g., headache or backache; any unfamiliar ailment will quite readily be dismissed. At times you take things too literally and can thus get hurt quite easily. You will, however, hide these feelings, and this can be confusing for your lover. You have a very good memory for what you consider essentials, but day-to-day obligations (taking your partner out to dinner, or to a doctor) can be forgotten, so it is a good idea, perhaps even a necessity, to write these things down. You are not the most imaginative lover but you have good staying power!

As a parent You were, or are, probably a good student, who enjoys reading and study, and you will expect the same from your offspring. You may be disappointed if your children are less academic than you were, and creative and sporting skills will not be given the notice or

40

praise they deserve. However, you are a caring person and communicate well when approached at the right time. You do not inspire confidence.

DISCONNECTED

To wish You a very happy Christmas an a New Year.

You are very intuitive and show an unusual insight into the minds and motives of other people. You react on first meeting with either approval or disapproval, rarely changing your mind at a later date. You are very individualistic and are often fascinated by the unusual – that is, as long as the idea appeals. As you tend to have a 'grasshopper' mind, your interests and ideas can change quite readily. Normally, your type are collectors of rare and unusual objects. Emotionally, you are sensitive and need time alone to protect yourself from over-stimulation. But you can be moody, restless, antisocial, selfish, and very critical of others, without much insight into your own moods and motives.

In business   Your critical faculty can be very useful, and you would make a very good theatre or film critic. Keen observation and a great memory for impressions are two of your talents. You have great imaginative potential, inspirational and innovative thoughts and ideas; you may enjoy writing stories and poetry. Your instinctual reactions can result in violent, verbal outbursts, making it difficult for you to work in a team but, left to your own devices, you can produce ideas or works of great originality. At other times, you may demonstrate an erratic kind of thinking that leads nowhere.

As a lover   You're original, lively and imaginative if your lover is in favour; but otherwise totally disinterested. Your desires vary from feelings of tender love to just plain lust. You can be turned on by a moonlight walk or walking in the mud, and are provocative and stimulating. You are a great animal lover too and may invite Rufus (the dog) or Sam (the cat) to share the bed with you. You want material possessions, but do not need them. You may offer your lover instead the first daffodil of spring, a beautifully coloured stone from the beach, or even a poem written especially for them. Are you prepared to go backpacking in outer Mongolia to see the apes? If you are the stay-at-home type, avoid the disconnected writer; they will not settle for the mundane. Despite their somewhat selfish natures, these people attract others from all walks of life and are rarely short of friends. Nice to have around.

As a parent You take an interest in everything the children have to say and do: yours is the household where the children's drawings are hung all over the fridge door and possibly up the staircase as well. Conker-collecting, nature rambles, picnicking and camping could all be part of their upbringing, and family pets will feature strongly. Each child in this household will be treated as an individual and their strengths and weaknesses handled accordingly.

TOTALLY DISCONNECTED (cursive or print)

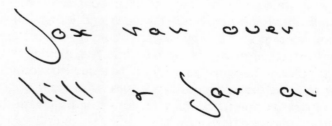

You have difficulty in understanding yourself and other people. You may be introverted and have feelings of inadequacy, a loner who can be both competitive and rebellious. You tend to have a dislike of authority figures, and normal rules and regulations. Your reactions are instinctive and you are very quick to jump to conclusions. Always critical and aloof, you experience great difficulty in linking experiences to meaningful direction. You can be inconsistent in your behavioural patterns, and behave in an immature manner. Invariably, your type is very self-centred.

In business You will be competitive in whatever you decide to work at, but you much prefer to work alone and unsupervised. You strive for perfection and are often disappointed that you do not attain the high standards you set for yourself. You like to work when you feel like it, rather than be committed to specific times. You are likely to be particularly good at working with your hands and would make a superb carpenter, builder, mechanical engineer or decorator.

As a lover You share time with your partner as and when you want to, and quite often choose to be alone. Though you feel quite empty at times, you rarely admit this to those who care for you. Basically, you are not co-operative, and are mean with social overtures. At times your antisocial behaviour is such that your partner will feel more comfortable socializing alone, as you are unaware of your unreasonable behaviour. Sexually, you need ego-boosting and confirmation that you are the best, the one and only. Trust does not come high on your list of character traits.

As a parent You are inconsistent, wavering between showing a lot of care and not being around because you are following your own pursuits. As you loathe being tied down or committed, any limitations the children impose, such as the need for babysitters, will irritate and receive little consideration. You find it difficult, not to say impossible to adapt your behaviour to suit a situation and

43

have a complicated and strained relationship with your partner and your children.

WORDS SOMETIMES CONNECTED

it says I am a ought not to find it

You have an avant-garde type of creativity and originality. You are exacting in your business transactions but have blind spots in your concentration. You see openings and opportunities that others miss, but can be careless about detail. You possess intense mental energy, love completing crosswords and studying languages; you may have an interest in creative writing. You also enjoy many cultural interests, such as art, literature and music.

6

Letter Shapes

m	mmmmmm	ARCADE
w	uuuuuuu	GARLAND
M	MMMMM	ANGULAR
~	~~~~~	THREAD
m	∞∞∞∞∞∞∞	ROUNDED

ARCADE

*I am 18 years old and fc
the past 2½ years, since leav
school I have been training tc*

You are slow to accept change unless it is gradual, a traditionalist who is very protective of everything. Screening your thoughts and bottling your feelings comes naturally to you. You tend to shut out the outside world and have a strong dislike of consulting others about what you consider to be your business. You treat your home as a place of security from the outside world and can be overly secretive. You are a serious person who takes a long time to make a decision but adheres strictly to it once made.

In business Your perseverance may lead to your becoming head of an organization. You can be slow to learn but once something is learned, it is never forgotten. You are very fair, and could well be a talented public speaker.

You don't allow anyone to dominate you, and you get along well with most people, but on the whole you are reserved and can be somewhat sceptical. Many of your type display an artistic sense of proportion and can be creative in a practical sense. Your emotions are well controlled.

As a lover Though you are quite warm and affectionate, you don't often show it, either emotionally or sexually. You are very loyal to those you trust but it can take a long time for you to commit to a long-term relationship. You appreciate quality paintings, sculptures and handcrafted articles. You show good taste and will invest in items expected to increase in value. You may be musically talented or, at least, show great appreciation of music. You are in no way given to fickleness and tend to remain with partners for life.

As a parent Naturally reserved, you do not like your children to discuss your business away from home. You enjoy the security of married life and welcome a few, well-chosen friends to your home. Your children will probably have a small circle of friends, whom you have approved. They will be encouraged to work hard to achieve their full potential. Over-indulgence is not likely to feature, either emotionally or materially, but a good standard of education will be a goal, with university or technical training if appropriate.

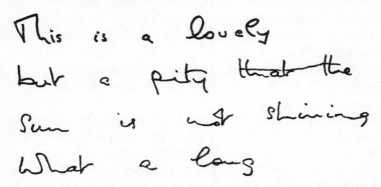

This is a lovely
but a pity that the
Sun is not shining
What a long

You are the easy-going type, and invariably remain pleasant and obliging. Generally you are passive and try hard to avoid arguments or confrontation. You adapt easily to changes in circumstance and are very sensitive to atmosphere. You are at your happiest when entertaining in your own home and make an excellent host or hostess. It is very important to you to be accepted by others and you can actually go overboard in your attempt to be liked. Genuine niceness, kind-heartedness and charm, together with a sympathetic disposition, all go to make you a particularly pleasing individual.

In business You may have considerable ability in your chosen career (check other writing movements), but your motto is: 'Be nice to everyone on the way up; you just might meet them on the way down'. Some of your type have particular ability in jobs relating to the worlds of art and literature. You are extremely approachable and will always be prepared to listen to others' viewpoints. However, others would be ill-advised to pick a quarrel with you – you will literally run, or take to your sickbed, until things return to normal.

As a lover Open, warm, and receptive, with a responsive nature, you treat your partner with affection and thoroughly enjoy the lover/husband/wife role. Nothing gives you greater pleasure than to be surrounded by your loved ones, at family parties, weddings, christenings – and you will always be prepared to do all the catering. Romance and thoughtfulness are part of your overall character. So if someone wants flowers regularly, or return visits to special places, you would be an ideal partner for them.

As a parent You are loving and caring but too passive; the children tend to run rings around you. They soon learn to do what they like, knowing full well that you will not confront them or do anything that will lead to arguments in the home. You may leave too many things unsaid, so that your children cannot easily recognize their boundaries. However, since you and your husband or wife will invariably have a very happy life together after your offspring have 'flown the nest', your children will always be welcomed home. You are the type to feel very disappointed if your children cannot be around you at Christmas or on your birthday. You will make an excellent grandparent.

ANGULAR

believe is your change for a full report. I don't have any specific questions to ask, + unfortunately can't provide an earlier sample.

Determined and competitive, you thrive on hard work and problem-solving. You can be inflexible, but show a high degree of maturity and mental energy. Nothing delights you more than being in command and on top of a situation. You demonstrate independence of spirit as well as the ability to keep your emotions under control. You make a good leader but have great difficulty with any form of compromise. You have an aptitude for thoroughness and practical application, and you are idealistic, with a probing mind that wants answers, even to the inexplicable. You can be very sarcastic.

In business You are positive, ambitious and work extremely hard to achieve your aims. Such is your determination that you will invariably reach the top of your profession. Some might call you hard, and you certainly set high standards, both for yourself and for others. You have limited patience for waffling and petty excuses and expect others to come straight to the point. A great individualist, you know what you want and how to get it. You are self-critical, analytical and logical, with a love of computers.

As a lover Human emotion baffles you, so a lover's appeals to you must be based on logic. You save your affection for your partner rather than for the children, home or family pet. Often you appear reserved, but can be possessive and jealous. If you encounter any major problems in a relationship, you will make every effort to sort it out, but you can't be bothered with trivial problems, such as the broken-down washer or vacuum cleaner! You can be a very aggressive lover and quite imaginative, but, at times, you may appear cold, indifferent or preoccupied. The most up-to-date piece of technological equipment is a prized gift here.

As a parent Encouraging but tough, you adopt an air of control and discipline which pervade the household. You do not like the children staying in bed late or sitting around doing nothing; instead you encourage activity – game-playing or sports. You welcome questions and will do your best to answer them truthfully. On the whole, you are a good parent, if perhaps a little strict at times. You encourage job-taking during holidays and show a great deal of pride in academic success.

*Today we are at sea having
spent two very hectic days in
Leningrad.*

Normally you are diplomatic and mix very well with all types of personalities. You dislike arguments and solve problems by compromise rather than argument. Adaptability, versatility and impressionability are all characteristics of yours, though you can be evasive and deceitful. You don't like being limited to a particular course of action and if you are, you are likely to make a number of changes *en route*. Your writing shows high intelligence and a love of the arts. Socially you can be inconsiderate and difficult to understand. Your concentration is often divided and you are susceptible to influences from others. Favouring appreciation rather than material gain, yours is a highly interesting type.

In business As tact and diplomacy are strong traits, you can be very useful to have around, but there is no guarantee that you will be around when others need you. However, you are extremely charming and often sublimate your own creative talents in order to bring them out in others. Your ideas are original and your intellect keen. You may be a lecturer, a teacher, or work in a charitable capacity. Broadminded, you rarely frown on anyone.

As a lover You are really quite charming, tender and loving, but not always as truthful or reliable as one might wish – you may well change appointments, or arrangements, at the last moment. You have a wide variety of changing interests, and are happy to include those close to you in your outings. You are curious about a great many things, and a love of art comes high on your list as do wining, dining and exotic foods. You give colourful descriptions of places you have visited and can transport listeners with your descriptive tales. It is easy for others to forgive you for many of your weaknesses, as your positive traits compensate for so much.

As a parent You may spoil your children but you also open their minds to many things. You listen to their ideas, encourage and praise their endeavours and intuitively know how to handle the different personalities within the household. At times, you do not make yourself available to do things when promised, but you try to compensate by arranging exciting outings. Your ideas are as numerous as your mind is open.

ROUNDED

close an addvessed
k and hope that you
ply if you are not to

It is considered unusual for an adult to write in this way but perfectly normal for a teenager. Immaturity is shown, as is the need for reassurance. Not a good decision-maker, you tend to discuss your problems with all your friends before reaching a conclusion – then you are likely to change the decision, again and again. You can be very emotional and go overboard for very minor reasons. Jealousy and possessiveness are frequently close to the surface, and you may create scenes in public. You have a great desire for security, yet find it difficult, whatever the circumstances, to feel secure. Constant reassurance is needed here, and others do tire of your demands.

In business   You can be very lazy and self-indulgent, working when you want to but finding all sorts of excuses for not completing a certain task or project. It is never your fault: 'The figures weren't available' or 'The computer isn't working properly' – anything to save your skin. You are very childish. Fortunately, very few adults write with a totally rounded script.

As a lover   'How many times have I told you I love you?' could well be your partner's most frequent remark. Sexually you are very eager, but then self-doubt settles upon you again. You are very kind, and would give a lover everything you own, but you want to own them too – you want their heart, mind, soul and body, and that can be very difficult for your lover to handle. This is expected, perhaps, at 15 – but not when we reach our adult life. You may love showering gifts on your lover, but again, it is because you are seeking approval. You can become very upset and emotional if your lover forgets to acknowledge your birthday or anniversary.

As a parent   You over-indulge them – almost like a child caring for children. You are very protective towards them and will fight anyone who threatens the security of any family member, but, in all other ways you prefer compromise to argument. Your children will be beautifully dressed and fed whatever they desire, but little discipline will be exercised. Rarely will they be denied the latest toys or clothes. Of course, this makes them brattish. It is too important for you to keep up with the Joneses.

7

Writing Styles

Simplified

Original

loopy

Ornate

SIMPLIFIED

sleeping area .

.... and it was

so that the new bedroom

down to the lower tier

You like a direct approach to everything and strive to simplify issues. You may be highly intelligent but you can also be very impatient. You have a quick grasp and assimilation of essentials, a bias towards reserve, discretion and matter-of-factness. As you invariably have a high degree of energy and a very quick mind you are capable of reaching great heights. However, you do not like others to disagree with you and make a poor listener. You are disciplined and a great go-getter.

In business You show many leadership qualities and are probably (or will be) at the top of your chosen profession. Capable of easily distinguishing the important from the unimportant, you work at a great speed. You are a happy mixture of imagination and intelligence which enables you to make your dreams come true. You can be intolerant of others who do not grasp facts as quickly as you do and they will be left in no doubt as to how you feel about them, for you will say it straight to their face! You admire achievement and will encourage those you consider deserving of your time and energy.

As a lover Without an intelligent partner, you will soon be bored to tears. Cocktail parties have no appeal as you cannot tolerate small talk, but invite some academics, writers, artists, or others at the top of their field, around for dinner and you will be in your element. Your directness can get you into trouble socially, as you speak your mind much too readily. Sexually you are active but have a fairly clinical approach and cut out the preliminaries. You love beautiful, expensive things and have a strong dislike of gaudy or shoddy goods. Vulgarity has little appeal for you and loud music offends you. You are cultured, have good taste and enjoy reading.

As a parent You make a good, caring parent but like to impose your ideas on your children. You don't listen sufficiently to them so their aims and ideas can get pushed into the background. You are probably very proud of 'the old school tie', and want your children to attend the same school. You will have difficulty in accepting the chosen partners of your children, as nobody is ever considered good enough for them.

ORIGINAL

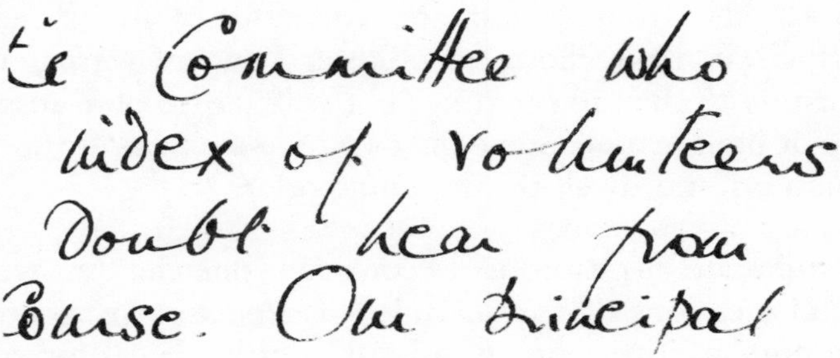

[handwritten text]

You have a creative, original mind, rich in ideas, as well as good visual sense and imagination. Invariably, you are animated but you are also a generally relaxed type who has no difficulty in relating with others. You may at times appear boisterous or even boastful, but are very big-hearted and always pleasant to have around. You can be greedy for sensation and have a love of the spectacular; at times you are emotional but you are predominantly charming, with an excellent visual memory.

In business Providing you are employed in an artistic field you do extremely well. Your artistic leanings, visual mind and love of colour can lead you into jobs involving design, creating patterns involving colour, producing book illustrations or book covers – all of these areas provide outlets for your talents. Often your type work in less creative jobs, but if you have outlets in your hobbies for your many talents, you will enjoy life; otherwise you can become quite depressed.

As a lover You have plenty of imagination and a colourful and light-hearted approach to life. You become depressed in tasteless surroundings and are at your most exuberant when surrounded by what you consider beautiful. A nature-lover, you love a partner to share the changing faces of the seasons with you. Your mind is rich in ideas and you can be adventurous and daring. Never one to conform, you find pleasure in exploring life and originality, either alone or with a chosen partner. Colour means a great deal to you and you will attempt to influence partners in their choice of clothes. You are warm, and ardent with the right partner, but will get rid of a possessive or limiting one. Sometimes you are awkward in social situations and dwell on the unimportant.

As a parent You probably consider your children wonderful creations of nature and will expose them to creative pursuits. Strict organization has little appeal for you, so getting the children to bed at a reasonable hour, or feeding them on time, will not be an issue; nor are you terribly practical. Hugs and kisses will rarely be in short supply but goodies for the packed lunch might be!

LOOPY

Please find enclosed my cheque. I hope we will meet soon.

The dominance of loops indicates a very emotional person: not only do you respond in an emotional fashion but you need an emotional response from others. This can seem vain, immature and hypersensitive, but it also indicates a sympathetic and compassionate nature. You may appear to be extroverted while actually feeling insecure inside. You are talkative, impulsive and hedonistic.

In business You become deeply involved, whether it be

with customers, patients or colleagues, and find it difficult to maintain the boundary between your business and personal lives. Since you talk too much, you are not suited to positions where confidentiality is an important requirement; you loathe solitary occupations and need to be surrounded by others. You are undoubtedly gifted with a good degree of intelligence but you dislike work where intense concentration is required. You waver between caution and independence and can be difficult to pin down.

As a lover The wider the loops of your script, the more gregarious and pleasure-seeking you are. You have a great need to be loved and find life barren if you aren't at the core of someone's existence. You love having a fuss made of you romantically. You also love music, movement, dancing and rhythm. Sexually you are very experimental – more or less anything goes. But you can be emotionally draining to your partner, wanting their full attention. Basically you are only attracted to very lively personalities and find the quiet type boring.

As a parent Full of cuddles and giggles, you more often than not welcome and enjoy the whole experience of parenthood. You go overboard about your 'gifted' or 'very beautiful' children, but are always sympathetic to their difficulties and problems, and will encourage them to be adventurous. Their friends will be welcome in the home and happily entertained, with lavish parties on birthdays, and plenty of loud music. You will dash off impulsively on some pursuit and children may well have to wait till late evening for supper, but no one seems to mind; you don't live by the clock. It's a pretty relaxed household.

If your handwriting is fussy or tremendously elaborate, it shows an emphasis on unimportant things. You can be vulgar – wearing brash or tasteless clothes – and boastful. You may be lighthearted, but are also vain and conceited. You probably wear too much make-up, drive a mauve or pink car, and have a garden full of gnomes in every conceivable colour. You can be very generous and insist guests eat everything put down in front of them, but you will also ply them with drinks, heedless of the consequences of drinking too much. You are adventurous, and always kind to your friends – but ghastly if you don't like someone, and often a noisy neighbour.

In business Best left to your own devices, you are almost certainly most suited to self-employment. You are likely to be at the races when an important meeting is being held and will even wonder why it cannot be changed to fit in with your social needs. Very ostentatious, you are boastful and tell wild stories; you are certainly not the most honest and are good at bending the truth. Your colleagues will always have a good time with you but will rarely trust you.

As a lover Do you wear very low-cut dresses or underwear saying 'welcome'? Maybe even condoms that smell of strawberries or liquorice? Maybe you paint all your nails a different colour. Your type has a bawdy sense of humour and you are fond of playing practical jokes which can be tasteless. Does innuendo creep into every word you utter? Are you very generous, sending 200 red roses to the one you love when they could far more easily accommodate a dozen? These are all acts of an extremely ornate writer. You will certainly embarrass your friends but, if they are the same type you could all be in for an interesting time. There is always fun in the bedroom, but not necessarily of an appropriate nature!

As a parent   Your children will tend to look like a mini-Mum or Dad, dressed to kill in all the latest fashions and the gaudiest colours. You'll lavish pocket money on them and they will learn at an early age to spend, spend, spend. Not much discipline is exercised in this home and children learn not to show much consideration to others; their manners are frequently sadly lacking. More often than not, they are encouraged to partake in a large range of activities.

8

Width of Strokes

Broadness   n m

Narrowness   n m

BROADNESS

*I absolutely don't
as what to write but
'l try to put something*

Broadness reveals someone who is expansive in social situations but can be quite contained in other areas of their life. You tend to be vivacious, sympathetic and generous, with broad views and a need to be free and unfettered. You are the world's best traveller and enjoy the whole experience, right from the moment you start your packing. Faraway places have great appeal – you feel drawn to the world and open spaces; you also need large rooms in which to spread yourself, and invariably have many and varied interests and hobbies. You can be very talkative and exaggerate stories. You like good clothes and enjoy mixed company. You are very frank, and friendly and helpful to those around you. You are also susceptible to others' charm.

In business The 9-to-5 type job is not for you, as you become extremely restless in this suitation. You give a great deal of consideration to the claims of others around you, helping colleagues whenever possible. Your aim in life is to be as good at your work as you can possibly be; you are deeply affected by failure and are driven to perfection by success. You have a good imagination but your ability to concentrate wavers: when it is good, it is extremely good, but at other times it is weak. Your eye for beauty often leads you to the world of design, fashion, and beauty, especially when travel is involved, but watch for a tendency to exceed your budget.

As a lover Adventurous and broadminded, your motto might be 'anything goes'! You easily attract others but are difficult to hang on to; you need romance, excitement and variety. Your ability to mix well makes it easy for you to associate with all types, from the penniless artist or writer to the successful head of an organization. Your impatience can get you into trouble. You will require a lot from your partner in terms of luxuries, but you are very generous, too – to your partner, friends and family, mentally and materially, and in all ways.

As a parent A child of yours is likely to be strapped to your chest when only a few weeks old, and shown the beauty of nature and the outside world. Exploration is what life is all about and this idea will be instilled in your offspring. They will be taken to restaurants, cinemas theatres, and concerts at an early age. The neighbours' children will be welcome in your home as well, and your children will enjoy a lively home life.

I am rather shy. I like going to
see the sort of people who have
and I play in an orchestra. My
reluctant but I can't afford it
is to learn to ski. I have a

To understand the character of a person with a very narrow script it is easiest to think of a curtain pulled back very tightly. You are narrow-minded, with narrow visions and a controlled personality. You limit yourself unnecessarily due to fear: the car might break down, the weather might change, the train will not get into the station on time. Your introversion is related to your inhibitions, which give rise to cautiousness and feelings of timidity and loneliness. You want everything neat and tidy and are either economical or just plain mean, avoiding unnecessary expense and hoarding whatever you can. Narrowness means the emotions are directed inwards, and you lose out on many of the joys of life.

In business You restrict yourself greatly and are frequently distrustful of the moods and motives of others. You do have a marked sense of duty and will stick rigidly to your promises. You work to a well-devised, predetermined plan and have great difficulty with improvising. You are very self-conscious and have a strong dislike of being observed when working. Both critical and analytical, you tend to work best in a technical capacity. You have strong ethical leanings.

As a lover Your sensitivity gives rise to problems and you behave in a modest and reserved manner. Your love-making can be quite mechanical and restrained, as your narrow-mindedness restricts any form of adventurous behaviour. Your lover will have few surprises, sexually or otherwise. You can be so predictable that bedtime boredom easily settles in. Nor do you have a flair for gift-giving. Sadly, a poverty of ideas does not help, but a warm, affectionate partner could.

As a parent You love your children but are over-protective, cautious and limiting. Your home will be beautifully kept, and your children will be well fed and clothed, but restricted in their movements. You may be too fearful to allow them to travel by train, go on school outings or stay at friends' homes for the night. However, these concerns are borne of an admirable, marked sense of duty to your children.

Pressure on Stroke

‒‒‒‒‒‒‒‒‒‒‒‒‒‒‒‒‒‒‒‒‒‒‒‒‒‒

‒‒‒‒‒‒‒‒‒‒‒‒‒‒‒‒‒‒‒‒‒‒‒‒‒‒

‒‒‒‒‒‒‒‒‒‒‒‒‒‒‒‒‒‒‒‒‒‒‒‒‒‒

‒‒‒‒‒‒‒‒‒‒‒‒‒‒‒‒‒‒‒‒‒‒‒‒‒‒

⋀ ⋀ ⋀ ⋀ ⋀ ⋀ ⋀ ⋀ ⋀

‒‒‒‒‒‒‒‒‒‒‒‒‒‒‒‒‒‒‒‒‒‒‒‒‒‒

Assessing Pressure

The degree of force can be judged by feeling an original sample of writing between your thumb and index finger. Strong indentation indicates heavy pressure; slight indentation indicates medium; no indentation indicates light. Pasty pressure looks heavy but has no indentation, and is frequently produced by a felt tip or broad nib. Light pressure with pointed tops is classified as sharp, and varying is a combination of both light and heavy.

HEAVY

It has been a pleasure you, and I hope you

Heavy pressure reveals a forceful personality with a great deal of energy available. No 'shrinking violet', you need to make an impression and are easily excited to action. You are not easily discouraged and can inspire others. Challenges are welcome, as is material reward for your efforts. Essentially you are materialistic, strong-willed and stubborn. Your remarkable energy is accompanied by great stamina, and you love change, new surroundings and active people. You can, however, be morose or given to depression. There is a tendency to indulge in anti-social or aggressive behaviour if you have insufficient outlet for your energies.

In business Powerful, strong and hard working, you welcome all new challenges with delight. You might be an excellent managing director or a particularly good salesperson. Rejection doesn't worry you unduly; you just go back for more. You can be both harsh and stern and sometimes others find it difficult to get along with you, but you are respected for your abilities and forceful attitudes: you certainly make your presence felt.

As a lover Extremely warm, ardent and demanding, you love company and can be tiring in your thirst for new experiences and love of activity. You need outlets for your physical energy, and your personality type often make good sports people. You enjoy wining and dining, travel, and are a very interesting companion, but you do demand attention. Sexually you are adventurous, extremely tactile and sensual. When frustrated you can be very aggressive.

As a parent You chivvy the family into activity but take your role as a provider very seriously. You like the trappings of wealth: big house, car, holidays, good education, and more. You can be intolerant and very stubborn, so the family tends to go along with your ideas. Your strong idealism can put pressure on your partner and offspring. Yours is never a boring household, and an unadventurous partner would never survive in this relationship. You can be aggressive, or even cruel, to your offspring.

MEDIUM

I used to buy pens all the time, usually fountain pens so that

This pressure is the most common one seen, and an indication of a reasonable degree of energy and vitality. If you use medium pressure, you are the adaptable type, with a primary interest in people, and a secondary interest in material things. You have sufficient willpower to overcome problems or obstacles on a day-to-day basis and do not try to impose your will on others.

In business You have a reasonable drive and do not necessarily want to extend yourself too far. As you are both adaptable and composed you tend to be popular with your colleagues. You listen to and help others: people-handling is one of your gifts.

As a lover Providing you do not have an over-demanding partner, you are loving, caring and pleasant. You enjoy most things in moderation and are consistent in your behaviour. There is no point in others surprising you with expensive gifts; you will only worry about the extravagance of the deed!

As a parent Nurturing and thoughtful, you will expect only what you consider the children are capable of. You will get to know other parents and help at school fêtes and the like. You are considered nice but unadventurous.

When I returned to the city, where I had been born, after many years of absence I was dismayed to find that many of it's narrow streets had been.

Light pressure shows a person with low energy levels and stamina. You are sensitive and greatly affected by things others do and say. You take offence easily, even when none was intended. You have a certain delicacy of feeling and can be greatly upset by violence and swearing, on television or elsewhere in your environment. You loathe loud noises, blaring radios, rough behaviour and harsh words. You may experience difficulty in learning from past experiences and tend to repeat your mistakes. You are likely to be idealistic, with an interest in spiritual development, refined, gentle and sensitive to beauty, art and music.

In business You are at your best working in a creative field and, being very idealistic, set high standards for yourself. If you choose to work in a sales organization you will have the necessary intelligence, but as you are not aggressive you will have to work twice as hard as the person who writes with heavy pressure, as those writers more naturally succeed in this area. This type of work could take its toll on your delicate nature and result in your being rather tense and nervous. Your thoughts and feelings are intense, but they do not last for long. You would make a good television or theatre critic.

As a lover You are extremely gentle and tender. As you love the arts, you will want a partner who will accompany you to art galleries, theatres, concerts, and the like. Your sensitive nature needs careful handling and you take offence if for some reason an arrangement is cancelled.

You have a low tolerance for alcohol, so should not over-indulge; neither do you react well to shock or drugs. Your love of beauty is tremendous and, if you find the right person, you will treat them like a precious object. The sex will be sparing but very tender.

As a parent You encourage your children to behave beautifully at all times, to show consideration for others and refrain from shouting or raising their voices. Your children grow up aware of many cultural pursuits and will consider this a normal way of life. You will welcome the 'right' friends for your children into your home, but you will be very selective. Often the children of your personality type are successful as actors, since they experience little difficulty in taking on the character of another person while leaving their own hidden.

PASTY

I would like to study Graphology further. Is there a course offered here in

A pasty pressure appears heavy, but is in fact light. The heavy look is produced by a felt-tip or broad-nibbed pen consciously chosen for its effect, and the style is always indicative of a marked prevalence of sensual traits. You delight in creature comforts that stimulate the five senses: perfume, food and drink, touching, music and movement. You have a deep appreciation of the present moment but also welcome new experiences. You exhibit genuine warmth and a good sense of humour. You try to make life fun and are a very good companion. You are deeply emotional and carry the scars of hurt or happiness for a long time. You need richness and luxury in your life but hate losing money. You are a nature lover with particular love of flowers and trees.

In business You usually delight in a free and easy disposition which enables you to get along very well with colleagues. Your deep appreciation of colour and a marked aptitude for working with it would make you an excellent photographer, designer, or artist. You have a gifted imagination and an ability to visualize. But this can lead to day-dreaming or, on other occasions, burning out by endeavouring to do too much at once.

As a lover You are extremely warm, sensual and ardent. Dining out or cooking exotic meals at home plays an important part in your routine. Good wines are also greatly appreciated but – a word of warning – you can be given to excesses! Walking in the woods by moonlight or tramping through the countryside all have appeal. You look on the positive side of life and have a great sense of fun. You will surprise your lover with well-chosen gifts at any time: 'Why wait for birthdays?' is your attitude. You need tasteful surroundings and attractive companions. But keep away from casinos – you hate losing! You're a very sexy partner, who enjoys buying a lover flowers or perfume.

As a parent You are very interested in your offspring and will delight in taking them for nature rambles (imparting information as you go), or sailing trips and travel at home and abroad. You give generously of your time, feelings and ideas, exuding warmth and offering plenty of kisses and cuddles. Yours may not be the most organized household but it's among the happiest. Here, the children are always encouraged to use their imaginations.

All goed men came to the and of the party

You experience emotions intellectually rather than with the whole body. You tend to be hypersensitive and nervous, an idealist with very high morals and principles, and you see things as right or wrong, good or bad, pure or sordid. When you choose to communicate you are articulate and rapid in speech. You are a deep thinker but your feelings are not long-lasting. You may be spiritual, and are very sensitive to beauty in all its forms. You don't have an abundance of energy but tend to save it for when it is necessary. Scepticism and an analytical mind are other character traits found in your type. You can be extremely critical, with a hasty temper.

In business On the whole, you are clever, critical and logical. You set very high standards and are never content with low work-standards or poor time-keeping. You can subdue colleagues with a particular sense of humour that shows considerable irony and sarcasm. Under pressure, you become extremely irritable and nervous, so are best left to work at your own pace. You would make an excellent theatre or film critic; many clergymen and women produce this type of stroke.

As a lover You place a lot more emphasis on the importance of mental processes than emotions. You are very conscious of hygiene and dislike anything you might consider 'dirty'. You are not prone to over-indulgence in food, drink or sex, and you have a low tolerance for shock and drugs. You can be cold, remote and restrained. You are very selective in those you associate with and have a great dislike of any form of loudness or vulgarity. Sex, too, will be a matter for restraint.

As a parent Your children will be expected to obey all the household rules without question. If they follow the same refined, cultural pursuits that you do, everyone will be happy; but should the children be interested in more boisterous activities, you will show total disinterest. Energy is reserved in this family for what is considered refined, decent and respectable – with little room for manoeuvre! Hasty tempers do flare from time to time. An immaculately kept home is very important to you.

VARYING

told that sloping letters
: shows signs of distrust
ing upright!

If your handwriting is light on some strokes and heavy on others, it shows a personality that is still in the process of growth – varying between idealism and materialism, ardour and restraint. You can be optimistic one day and pessimistic the next. The majority of us develop one particular pressure eventually.

G. Bernard Shaw

Best wishes — Sue Lawley.

Margaret

Elizabeth R

Anne

Alexandra

Mark Phillips

Elvis Presley

Gary Lineker

Iza Goddard

Jacqueline Kennedy

Love
Paul McCartney

Sincerely
Bette Davis

Anita Dobson

Hugh M Hefner

WALT DISNEY

Tessa Sanderson

SECTION II

Secondary Movements

10

The Personal Pronoun: 'I'

	Form		Indicates
1	$\mathcal{I}$	Printed	Clear thinking, good taste, confidence
2	$9\,|$	Small (either printed or cursive)	Lack of confidence, a feeling of being hard done by
3	$9|$	Very tall	Confidence and pride
4	$|$	Single stroke	Intelligence, independent thinking
5	$\int$	Narrow loop	Idealism and emotional control
6	g	Average loop	Emotional well-being and good willpower
7	g	Very wide loop	Emotionalism, vanity and pride
8	∂	Closed	Total absorption in self

9	∂	Arc to left	Great difficulty in taking responsibility
10	g	Pointed at top	Desire for explanations for everything and a probing mind
11	4	Like Fig. 4	Inflexibility; irritability and defensiveness
12	1	Like Fig. 7	Familiarity with figures and a love of material possessions
13	9	Like Fig. 9	Influence of the father and early life experiences
14	2	Like Fig. 2	Feeling of being second-rate and difficulty in relating intimately (often has a particularly clever brother or sister)
15	∂	Small and cramped	Shyness and self-consciousness
16	i	Like small letter	Great immaturity and a crushed ego
17	4	Hook to the left	Aggressiveness and retention of negative feelings from the past
18	X	Like letter X	Fear of dying; fear of true nature being exposed

19	Triangular base	Hard and aggressive nature
20	Simplified with tick starting stroke	Concision and precision
21	Simplied with curved base	Independence and self-contentment
22	Amended	Temporary malaise and touchiness
23	Coiled	A love of self and a tendency towards greediness
24	Curved	Avoidance of involvement; can suggest hearing problems
25	Musical symbol	Musical appreciation or ability
26	Bowed to left	Invitation to others to treat you badly, either verbally or physically
27	Dropping below baseline	Insensitivity to partner's feelings; deceit
28	Top and bottom strokes disconnected	Active or passive participation in ball games

29		Unusual loops to left	Possible homosexuality
30		Lighter pressure than text	Uncertainty regarding identity and difficulty in fitting in with others
31		Heavier pressure than text	Feelings of aggression towards others
32		Written at different angle	Guilt complex
33		Attached to first word	Feelings of extreme loneliness; need for companionship
34		With large space before next word	Self-protectiveness and uncertainty in approaching a situation or person

11

The Sexual Area: 'g' & 'y'

		Form	Indicates
1	*g y*	Balanced and complete	Ability to be content and happy within one relationship; makes a loving partner
2	*q y g*	Very small lower stroke or loop	Little interest in sex; temporary fatigue
3	*g y*	Very narrow loop	Sexual repression; fear of commitment
4	*g y*	Very wide loop	Good sex drive and imagination; materialistic streak
5	*g y*	Unfinished loop	Flirtatious nature; lack of interest in the sex act
6	*g y*	Low crossing	Dissatisfaction with current partner

7	Swinging endstroke	Desire for constant change of partner
8	Long, straight stroke to left	Nature that derives a lot of pleasure from masturbation
9	Endstroke to left	Sublimated sexual urges; enjoyment in helping others
10	Small triangle	Sexual anxiety and frigidity, frustration
11	Large triangle	Sexual aggression combined with indifference to partner; tendency to leave partner frustrated
12	Very long, looped	Ease of emotional involvement; love of sporting activities
13	Hook to left	Avoidance of responsibility; will run from commitment
14	Completed figure 8 in lower zone	Possible homosexuality
15	Tick on endstroke	Need for encouragement and reassurance
16	Very heavy pressure and full loop	Sexually demanding nature (three times a day!)

17		Straight downstroke	Selfishness
18		Exaggerated lower zone movements	Active or latent homosexuality
19		Broken base	Sexual disappointment and fearful nature
20		Like a corkscrew	Inventiveness and imagination
21		Upstroke drops	Feeling of discouragement or anger towards partner
22		Loop on baseline	Sexual vanity (enjoys walking around naked)
23		Triangle in lower zone	Unresolved sexual anxiety; prudish nature
24		All *y*'s and *g*'s the same	Little imagination (every-Saturday-night type – preferably with the lights out)
25		Two or three varieties	Healthy, imaginative interest in sex

| 26 | Every *y* or *g* different | Easily stimulated nature; lack of control |

$z928978$

12

Capital Letters

	Form	Indicates
1	Tall	Self-respect, self-reliance and a healthy degree of confidence

Handwriting   Analysis

	Form	Indicates
2	Very tall	Pride, vanity and conceit; mistaken confidence when starting on a new project

Handwriting   Analysis

	Form	Indicates
3	Short	Modesty, slight uncertainty and hesitation before undertaking anything new

Handwriting   Analysis

	Form	Indicates
4	Very short	Lack of confidence; humility and tendency to stick with the 'tried and trusted'

Handwriting   Analysis

5		First hump larger	Pride and egoism
6		Second hump larger	Pride in family achievements; desire to be liked and accepted
7		End stroke extending under whole word	Expectation that others will hang on your every word; self-satisfaction
8		Extremely simplified	Ability to see essentials instantly; individualism, creativity, structural ability
9		Very broad	Generosity, open-mindedness and love of freedom
10		Very narrow	Uptight, reserved, careful nature, lacking in spontaneity
11		Printed capitals with cursive writing	Clear thinking; desire to get on with whatever is of interest at this moment
12		Large loop at beginning	Pomposity and a desire for attention (found in the writing of actors, politicians and salespeople)

13		Extended top stroke	Enterprising nature with a love of challenges
14		Starting with an additional stroke	Difficulty getting along with others; tendency towards obstruction
15		Starting stroke over whole word	Protective nature, especially with friends, family and colleagues
16		No starting stroke	Practicality; directness
17		Long, straight starting stroke	Resentment; tendency to blame others for misfortune
18		Garland starting stroke	Warmth, affection, caring nature with a desire for acceptance
19		Arcade starting stroke	Nature that is secretive, slow to change, traditional

20	*DRY* (handwritten)	Angled starting stroke	Aggression, feeling of being cheated; hostility
21	*Space after Capital* (handwritten)	Space after capital	Observant nature with the ability to sense atmosphere

13

Small Letters

	Form	Indicates
1	Variations of the same letter in a piece of writing	Versatility and adaptability
	⊢RS↗a2ee	
2	Missing letter in the middle of a word	Distraction, poor concentration; individual under pressure
	Crزy = Crazy brve = brave	
3	Missing letter at end of word	Mind working faster than the pen on paper; a desire to move on to next interest or project; impatience
	centr = centre modes = modest	
4	Letters decreasing at end of word	Tact and diplomacy; ability to keep a secret
	decreasing	

| 5 | Letters increasing at end of word | Blabbermouth; gossip |

increasing

| 6 | Capital in the middle of a word | Mistaken or confused priorities |

ciRcles

| 7 | A mixture of print and cursive | Social insecurity; sparing communication and discomfort in large groups |

tys' pant like this if it's my to a close friend. However,

| 8 | A mixture of broad and narrow letters | Broadmindedness, generosity alternating with nervousness, meanness |

Now is the time

| 9 | Reversed letters | Antisocial behaviour and a dislike of normal rules, regulations and people in authority |

$d = 6 \quad s = 2 \quad k = \lambda$

| 10 | Strokes that fall below the line | Stubbornness, obstinacy and firm convictions |

d ↑ k

| 11 | Elaborate letters | Vulgarity, coarseness and noisiness |

12	Letters tied in knots	Inflexibility

13	Lasso loops on letters	Poetic, childlike but pleasant nature

14	Curly strokes	Great sense of humour and a sense of the ridiculous

15	Angular letters	Determination, mathematical ability, thoroughness

16	Unusual letter formations	Originality, creativity and individualism

17	Ink-filled letters	Nature given to excesses; possibility of violence

18	Spiky tops	Probing mind, argumentative streak

19	Very small *i* in relation to other letters	Kindness; a feeling of self-pity (often found in the handwriting of nurses and carers)

Very tiny

20	With double letters, second taller than first	Ability to command respect on entering a room (teachers, lecturers)

el tt

21	Very large *a* and *o* in relation to other letters	Jealousy and possessiveness in relationships

cOmparison

22	Double circles on *a* and *o*	Tendency to be hypocritical and devious; possibility of dishonesty

a o

23	Letters open on baseline	Flexible morals; lack of trustworthiness

a o b

24	Very tall upper zone movements	Pride, high ideals and imagination

tall like this

25	Very low upper zone movements	Lack of imagination; dull personality

small like this

26	Constant amendments that do nothing to aid legibility	Neurotic tendencies; fear and suspicion

d   t   l   m

27	Letters like figures	Mathematical ability; good judgement.

$g = 9$ $r = 2$

$t = 7$ $y = 4$

28	Greek *e* and *d*	Refinement, culture (often found in the handwriting of writers and journalists)

29	Extra loops on *m* and *n*	False charm and flattery; also a concern for others

30	*a* and *o* open to left	Tendency to speak about others behind their back

31	*a* and *o* open to right	Open and direct nature

32	*d* curled back	Self-protectiveness; speedy replies

14

i Dots

		Form	Indicates
1	$\dot{\iota}$	Directly above	Precision, accuracy
2	$\iota\,^{\bullet}$	To the right	Impulsiveness, impatience
3	$^{\bullet}\,\iota$	To the left	Procrastination and caution
4	ι	Omitted	Lack of attention to detail, carelessness
5	$\overset{\bullet}{\iota}$	Very high	Curiosity, observant person
6	$\overset{\frown}{\iota}$	Arcade	Secretiveness, control
7	$\overset{\frown}{\iota}\;\overset{\frown}{\iota}$	Like dash	Hasty temper, irritability and sarcasm
8	$\overset{\sim}{\iota}$	Wavy	Fun-loving nature

9	.	Light	Weak will; lack of energy
10	•	Very heavy	Strong will, overbearing nature
11	◀	Club shape	Aggression, cruelty
12	○	Circle	Attention-seeking, slight eccentricity (often found in the writing of people who enjoy working with their hands - artists and craftsmen, physiotherapists, hairdressers, chefs, etc.)
13		Varying	Inconsistent behaviour and work patterns; liking for change and variety

15

t Crosses

		Form	Indicates
1	L	Cross omitted	Carelessness, absent-mindedness
2	t	Low cross	Difficulty in overcoming day-to-day obstacles; caution
3	t	Medium	Conscientiousness and courage
4	t	High	Bravery and tenacity
5	t	To the left	Procrastination
6	t	Low cross away from stem	Acceptance of challenge, impatience
7	t	Middle cross away from stem	Drive, initiative and impatience
8	t	High cross away from stem	Leader who takes charge

9	t	Pointing down	Contrary and obstinate nature
10	†	Cruciform	Fatalism; religious leanings
11	t	Very heavy pressure	Energy, domineering, selfishness
12	t	Very light pressure	Weak will, lack of confidence
13	ŧ	Double cross	Obsessive nature with the inclination to recheck everything
14	L	Cross above the stem	Someone with their head in the clouds; lack of realism
15	ℓ	Looped	Sensitivity, vanity
16	x	Wavy	Sense of humour and fun; a mimic
17	t	Club-like	Bad-temper and cruelty
18	L	Upward curve	Quick mind but very critical
19	⫫ ⫪	Angled	Obstinacy, stubbornness; strong opinions
20	ꝗ ⱷ	Loop knot	Persistence and love of challenge

21		Long stroke across double *t*	Protective towards family and friends
22		Convex	Self-discipline
23		Concave	Self-indulgence
24		Varying	Unreliable willpower and control; versatility and the ability to improvise

16

Line Spacing

AVERAGE

currently at university after enter journalism as my chosen lthough I have nue 'o' levels

Normal spacing shows the ability to think clearly and explain things to other people. You are discriminating in what you do and in your choice of friends. You invariably have a sympathetic nature and are a good judge of character.

WIDE

*)n Sunday the 9th October /
enerife with a friend, on
derstand that you are the*

You fear closeness with others and tend to set yourself above other people. You can create grandiose fantasies and put yourself on a pedestal; alternatively, you may

just harbour distrust and suspicions. You make extravagant gestures from time to time to other people, and are
also frequently generous to yourself.

NARROW

... you know for
- the standard of
ence, memory, vitality,
bilities, interests, etc.,
revealed through

You suffer from confused thoughts and ideas. The more
the lines run into each other, the more confused your
personality. You are constantly in need of expressing your
thoughts and ideas but experience great difficulty in putting
them into action. Your concentration is not good and
you are prone to accidents. You are lively and forceful
but you lack clarity of purpose. You may be tight-fisted.

17

Word Spacing

WELL BALANCED

It position and I w
a repat on him. les sec
are pre eminent. He wil

Your writing shows clarity of thinking and inner organization, an ability to deal flexibly with others and handle
your own thoughts and feelings well. You are methodical
and opportunist. You strive to express yourself clearly
and can become irritated if misunderstood. Intelligence,
maturity, good planning and good judgement are clearly
shown here.

WIDE

Mary had a little lam
Its feet were white a
And everywhere that

You loathe living in close proximity to others for fear of
others breathing down your neck. You are selective in

everything, from your choice of friends to tasks in hand. Others can find you aloof or at least reserved. You normally show courage, independence and generosity. You dislike asking others for favours and prefer to make your own decisions. You show a tendency to isolate yourself and believe, correctly or incorrectly, that you have difficulty in communicating with others. You will commit yourself to issues or projects you consider appropriate, rather than accepting what others try to force upon you.

NARROW

last year at college doing a degree we applied to firms for a ing However I don't know if

You are excessively friendly and may compete with others for attention. You mix indiscriminately and hate being left alone, even for reasonably short periods of time. You can often be very selfish, expecting others to give readily of their time while you are not prepared to do likewise. Impulsive, you will intrude on conversations, expecting to be welcomed. Tact is not your strong point. You overextend yourself in all areas of your life.

VERY UNEVEN

I have just returned from San with an artist and a ps thing quite interesting

You are rather hesitant and unsure of how to behave or what path to follow. You may seem rather arrogant, but this is a cover-up for your confused thoughts and ideas. At times you are friendly, at other times less so. You do not plan well and tend to fall into situations. You are difficult to organize, and often join clubs or committees on a whim, only to decide later that this is not what you really want.

18

Margins

BALANCED

PERHAPS I
SHOULD PHONE
ROBERT TO
MAKE SURE

You have a self-assured personality and know how to
adjust to fit in with prevailing circumstances. You handle
your relationships well.

WIDE LEFT

I LIKE TO SIT
WRITE BOT I
AM ALWAYS
IN A HURRY
RUSH, RUSH

You are attempting to move forward and are communicative. The future is more important to you than the past;
you try to learn from past experiences and mistakes.

WIDE RIGHT

> I RESIST CHANGE AND LIKE TO PLAN WELL IN ADVANCE FOR EVERYTHING I DO.

Tomorrow scares you a little and you like to plan things well in advance. You are uncertain of the future and resist change. Your sensitivity holds you back and you will stay in unsuitable relationships for fear of ending up on your own.

WIDE MARGINS ALL ROUND

> I DO FEEL ISOLATED BUT DO NOTHING ABOUT IT!

You feel isolated and need to get out more and meet new people. You are confined in too small a range of interests and need to be less concerned about holding on to things and more interested in extending yourself.

ABSENCE OF MARGINS / WRITING
IN THE MARGINS

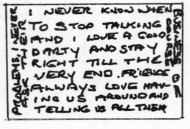

You are intrusive and do not recognize barriers between yourself and other people. At times, you become excitable and verbose. Give others their space and back off occasionally; not everybody can love you. You have a well-developed sense of economy.

DEEP TOP

I BELIEVE I RESPECT THE FEELINGS OF OTHERS. I CERTAINLY TRY.

You show respect for the feelings of others. Good timekeeping is important to you as you do not care to inconvenience others. You are quite formal, even reserved. You need to spend some time alone.

WHAT SHALL I
DO TODAY? I
JUST DON'T KNOW
MAYBE I SHALL
DECIDE LATER.

Your interest in other people quickly dissipates and you avoid commitment. You can be both idealistic and aloof, take offence much too readily and behave in a very sensitive manner. You don't always know what you want.

19

Signatures

A signature cannot be analysed on its own, but must always be examined in relation to the body of the script, as people often imitate the signature of someone they admire. An assumed signature frequently projects an image an individual would like to present to the world, and movements that appeal can be maintained for the extent of the signature but not for longer periods of time. People who sign many cheques or contracts may deform their signature, deliberately or unconsciously, to make it difficult for others to copy; similarly, those who sign vast amounts of correspondence may abbreviate their signature for speed.

	Form	*Indicates*
1	Text and signature identical	Lack of façade; the same behaviour in public and private

to know more about

I buy + are they esp

M Wilson

2	Larger	Uncertain ego; pretence of being extroverted

This is my usual script

Diana Jones

3	Smaller	A pretence of modesty; quiet confidence

Do you want this ?

Pamela Bridges

4	First name and surname connected	An ability to project your personality well; memorable character

Joan Collins

5	Rising	Professional ambition and drive

Pamela Joan Ingram

6	Falling	Negative frame of mind

Brenda Potts

| 7 | Single underline | Love of being noticed; a fair degree of confidence |

John Howard

| 8 | Double underline | Desire for recognition, love of an audience |

Paul Winter

| 9 | Wavy underline | Fair degree of confidence without the expectation of being taken seriously |

Sharon Brown

| 10 | Light full stop | Liking for the last word; caution |

Nancy Thomas.

| 11 | Heavy full stop | Insistence on having the last word; stubbornness |

Julia Brackit.

12	Two full stops	Love of a good argument; a need to have the last word

P. J. Dodds ..

13	Encircled	Pushy, secretive nature with a desire to outwit others

Reg Wilson

14	Letters decrease in size	Tact and diplomacy; consideration for others

Robert Dunn

15	Letters increase in size	Impulsiveness and tactlessness

Mary Hacker

16	Very broad	Need for space; intrepid qualities

Alec Harrison

17	Very narrow	Fear, tension and nervousness

Pamla Bridges

18	Extended endstroke	Distrust of the moods and motives of colleagues or friends

Eileen Moran

19	Long garland starting stroke	Difficulty in getting down to a task; feelings of uncertainty

Philip Sawyer

20	Long angular starting stroke	Resentful; blaming

David Evan

21	Very large capitals	Great pride and idealism

Catherine Patterson

22	Small middle initial	Dislike of middle name

Amy B. Green

| 23 | Small first initial | Personal uncertainty; reliance on social status for recognition |

H. Hughes.

| 24 | Large first initial | Greater emphasis on self than partner; often suggests an unhappy relationship |

Joe Lyons

| 25 | Right slant text – left slant signature | Self-doubt and time wasting (usually temporary) |

to the right

. Janice Holmes

| 26 | Left slant text – right slant signature | Outward confidence but inward uncertainty |

I write like this

Robert Dooley

| 27 | Slanting in all directions | Moodiness, uncertainty and provocativeness |

Paddy Murphy

28	Overly ornate in relation to the text	An exaggerated sense of own importance; not always truthful

Just ordinary script
Evelyn Major

29	Simplified in relation to the text	Verbose and evasive; a tricky combination

Kinda Elaboriated.
Jessie James

30	Heavier pressure than text	Willingness to strive for what you want

Light Pressure
P.J. Lyons

31	Lighter pressure than text	Diminishing momentum

Very Heavy
O. J. Smith

32	Use of full first name rather than initial	Attempt to break down initial barrier in getting acquainted; a friendly disposition

Mary Evans

Elizabeth Taylor

Charles

John Major

Jimmy Savile

Andrew

Philip

Margaret Thatcher

Dustin Hoffman

Warm regards
John Wayne

Diana.

Sarah Ferguson.

Judith Chalmers